Essential Preparation for

UMAT

UNDERGRADUATE MEDICINE & HEALTH SCIENCES ADMISSION TEST

Series One

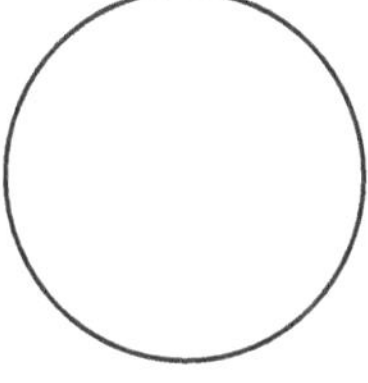

BOOK 1
LOGICAL REASONING & PROBLEM SOLVING

Mohan Dhall

Five Senses Education Pty Ltd
2/195 Prospect Highway
Seven Hills 2147
New South Wales
Australia

First Published 2013

Dhall, Mohan
Book 1 - Logical Reasoning & Problem Solving

ISBN 978-1-74130-771-9

CONTENTS

Introduction to UMAT and the Trial Test Papers

Students can gain access into medical training in Australia in one of three ways:

- Through post-graduate entry following the completion of an undergraduate degree. This degree should be in science or science related subjects and the student will need to achieve a high Grade Point Average (GPA)
- Through direct entry based on Year 12 results
- Through the UMAT test and interview

The purpose of an entry test is to assist in the selection of candidates who display the requisite skills and abilities for successful medical training. The three tests: logical reasoning and problem solving, understanding people and non-verbal reasoning assess a range of different types of cognition.

Supplementary to tests is an interview and thus interview skill and techniques should be practiced in addition to students undertaking test-training.

UMAT Trial Examination

Total Test Time: 180 minutes

Section 1: 48 Questions (70 minutes)

Section 2: 44 Questions (55 minutes)

Section 3: 42 Questions (55 minutes)

This book covers Section 1

Section 1 – Logical Reasoning and Problem Solving (70 minutes)

Number of questions: 48

Time allowed: 70 minutes

Instructions to candidates

Section 1 is a test of logical reasoning and problem-solving. There are 48 questions in this section.

Some of the questions rely on one piece of stimulus information that is provided. This may be presented graphically, in tabular form or in brief text pieces. For each question in this section you are to decide which of the four options given is the correct answer ***based only on the information provided***.

The questions assess your ability to comprehend, draw logical conclusions, reach solutions by identifying relevant facts, evaluate information, pinpoint additional or missing information, and generate and test plausible hypotheses.

Question 1

Blue-tongued lizards are the largest members of the skink family. Skink lizards have overlapping scales that are usually smooth and contain small plates of bone. The Eastern Blue-tongue is silvery-grey with broad dark brown or blackish bands across the back and tail. Individuals on the coast usually have a black stripe between the eye and the ear which may extend along the side of the neck. The Blotched Blue-tongue is dark chocolate brown to black with large pink, cream or yellow blotches on the back, and a tail banded in the same colours. The Eastern Blue-tongue can grow to almost 600 mm in total length, of which about 360 mm is head and body.

Blue-tongues maintain a body temperature of about 30°C - 35°C when active. During cold weather they remain inactive, buried deep in their shelter sites, but on sunny days they may emerge to bask.

Female blue-tongues give birth three to five months after mating, between December and April. The Eastern Blue-tongue usually gives birth between December and January. The embryos develop in the female's oviduct with the help of a placenta, which is as well-developed as that of many mammals. At birth the young eat the placental membranes and within a few days shed their skin for the first time. The young are ready to look after themselves straight after birth and disperse within a few days.

Reptile ticks are commonly found on blue-tongues; they attach under the scales and in the ear canal. They do not normally attach to mammals and are not known to cause paralysis. A number of nematode worms parasitise blue-tongues and may sometimes be seen in faecal pellets. Again, these worms normally only parasitise reptiles.

Adapted from http://australianmuseum.net.au/Eastern-Blue-tongue-Lizard

From this information it follows that

A) The blue-tongue scales are vulnerable to nematode worms
B) The tail of the Eastern Blue-tongue lizard can be over 300mm long
C) The Bob Tail Blue-tongue probably gives birth in summer
D) A baby blue-tongue born in January will be with its mother in February

Question 2

VO_2max is a measure of oxygen consumption. Scientists have tried to determine a relationship between VO_2max and running speed.

Predicted equivalent running times (hr:min:sec) for different racing distances related to predicted VO_2 max						
Maximum oxygen consumption (VO_2 max)	1500m	5km	8km	10km	21km	42km
93.6	(3.50)	10:00	(20:43)	(25:59)	55:52	01:56:02
89.9	(3:59)	11:00	(21:29)	(26:57)	57:59	02:00:37
82.7	(4:18)	13:00	(23:12)	29:07	01:02:46	02:05:34
79.1	(4:28)	14:00	24:11	30:21	01:05:27	02:10:57
75.5	(4:40)	15:00	25:14	31:43	01:08:23	02:16:48
71.9	(4:43)	16:00	26:23	33.08	01:11:55	02:23:12

Note: Running times that appear in brackets appear to be unrealistic. From CTM Davies and Thompson, 1979. Calculations by J. Affleck-Graves. Source: Lore of Running, Dr T Noakes, 1985, p68

To run a distance of 16 kilometres in a time close to 48 minutes the VO_2 max would most likely be which of these?

A) 89.9
B) 79.1
C) 82.7
D) 75.5

Question 3

In the suburb of Hannahia there are 2,000 children, half of whom are girls. 25% of girls play netball and 20% of the boys play cricket. 25% of the children receive private tutoring. 300 students play a sport and get tutoring.

How many children only play a sport and how many do no activities?

A) 700 and 800 respectively
B) 450 and 1500 respectively
C) 150 and 1350 respectively
D) 300 and 1500 respectively

Question 4

Consider the following table that shows key labour market trends over two months in 2012.

Key labour market figures 2012		
	October 2012	**November 2012**
Employed persons ('000)	11 529.4	11 535.2
Unemployed persons ('000)	647.8	648.5
Unemployment rate (%)	5.3	5.3
Participation rate (%)	65.1	65.1

Source: http://www.abs.gov.au/ausstats/abs@.nsf/mf/6202.0

According to the table,

A) Over time more people are getting jobs and more people are unemployed
B) Over time people are working longer hours
C) The number of people employed has risen by 5.8%
D) More people could expect to be unemployed in December 2012

Question 5

Four glasses, labelled A, B, C and D are on a table. Each is exactly half full of water. Two of the glasses can hold twice the volume of the other two glasses. The smaller glasses may be any two of A or B or C or D.

If the full content of glass B is poured into glass C, the full content of A is poured into glass D, half of D is poured into A and all of C is poured into D in that order then

A) Exactly a quarter of a small glass of water would spill
B) No water would be spilt if the small glasses are A and C
C) No water would be spilt if the large glasses are C and D
D) No water would be spilt if the large glasses are A and D

Questions 6 - 7

Researchers have found that a number of factors affected the buying behaviour of consumers purchasing a new car. A recent study interviewed 300 people and the results are shown in the table below. Note that two values (X and Y) are missing from the table.

Feature	Rated most important	Percentage	Rated least important	Percentage
Overall safety	59	20	**X**	2
Comfort	39	13	29	10
Brand	25	8	33	11
Design/look	27	9	35	11
Cost	94	31	24	8
Reliability	47	16	42	14
Power	9	3	131	**Y**
Total	**300**	**100**	**300**	**100**

Question 6

The missing values at X and Y should be, respectively,

A) 21 and 79
B) 6 and 44
C) 19 and 157
D) 79 and 42

Question 7

Which of the following would researchers be most justified in concluding?

A) Safety is a significant factor affecting consumer purchases
B) Comfort and safety are of roughly equal importance
C) On every measure cost is twice as important as reliability
D) The power of the motor vehicle is an insignificant consideration

Questions 8 - 10

Pertussis (whooping cough) is caused by the bacterium *Bordetella pertussis*. The disease is highly infectious and most serious in babies under the age of 12 months. Symptoms include coughing and 'whooping', which can continue for a few months. Complications of the disease include hypoxic encephalopathy (lack of oxygen to the brain) leading to brain damage and possibly death. Pertussis is a vaccine preventable disease. In Australia the take-up rate of the pertussis vaccine is very high, with around 95 per cent of children receiving the full three doses of vaccine by age two (at two, four and six months).However, pertussis infections in all age groups are on the increase globally. Australia recorded 38,000 cases in 2011, the highest number since records began in 1991 and most states are only now recovering from a major epidemic that began in 2008.

Researchers are still trying to understand why the vaccine does not totally protect against the infection. One possible explanation is that pertussis comes in a variety of strains and those strains change a lot over time. Associate Professor Stephen Lambert says an older version of the vaccine was more effective. Today's vaccine is known as an acellular vaccine; it does not contain whole cells of the whooping cough bacteria as the old vaccine did. Because of its side effects, the whole cell vaccine was abandoned in Australia in favour of the acellular vaccine.

Adapted from: http://www.health.gov.au/internet/immunise/publishing.nsf/Content/immunise-pertussis and http://www.abc.net.au/health/thepulse/stories/2012/08/14/3567495.htm#.UN7J3Y7rZFJ

Question 8

Which of the following is best supported by the information provided?

A) Most Australian children are fully vaccinated for whooping cough by age 18 months
B) Complications of whooping cough lead to brain damage
C) Newer vaccines are less effective than older vaccines
D) The number of whooping cough cases recorded in 2012 is around 41,000

Question 9

Which of the following statements is consistent with the information given?

A) Increasing the take-up rate of the pertussis vaccine should increase the incidence of pertussis infection in the general public
B) Vaccine preventable diseases cannot be prevented through vaccine use alone
C) Acellular pertussis vaccine has fewer side effects than whole cell pertussis vaccine
D) Doctors take months to effectively treat whooping cough

Question 10

From the information it follows that

A) Persons immunised with the acellular pertussis vaccine can catch whooping cough
B) Whole cell vaccines are always more effective than acellular vaccines
C) The pertussis bacterium mutates frequently which makes it difficult to vaccinate against
D) The pertussis vaccine will be 100 percent effective against whooping cough outbreaks if all people get vaccinated

Question 11

An old man and a young man are discussing the football over a cup of coffee. The old man comments, "I love Italian coffee". The younger man replies, "I love Vietnamese coffee". It is known that one of the men loves Italian coffee and the other man loves Vietnamese coffee. At least one of the men is lying.

Which of the following is correct?

A) The old man is telling the truth
B) The young man could not be lying
C) The old man does not like Vietnamese coffee
D) Both men are lying

Questions 12 - 14

A population of bacteria in a liquid medium is referred to as a culture. In the laboratory, where growth conditions of temperature, light intensity, and nutrients can be made ideal for the bacteria, measurements of the number of living bacteria typically reveals four stages, or phases, of growth, with respect to time. Initially, the number of bacteria in the population is low. Often the bacteria are also adapting to the environment. This represents the lag phase of growth. Depending on the health of the bacteria, the lag phase may be short or long. The latter occurs if the bacteria are damaged or have just been recovered from deep-freeze storage. After the lag phase, the numbers of living bacteria rapidly increases. Typically, the increase is exponential. That is, the population keeps doubling in number at the same rate. This is called the log or logarithmic phase of culture growth, and is the time when the bacteria are growing and dividing at their maximum speed. The explosive growth of bacteria cannot continue forever in the closed conditions of a flask of growth medium. Nutrients begin to become depleted, the amount of oxygen becomes reduced, the pH changes, and toxic waste products of metabolic activity begin to accumulate. The bacteria respond to these changes in a variety of ways to do with their structure and activity of genes. With respect to bacteria numbers, the increase in the population stops and the number of living bacteria plateaus. This plateau period is called the stationary phase. Here, the number of bacteria growing and dividing is equalled by the number of bacteria that are dying. Finally, as conditions in the culture continue to deteriorate, the proportion of the population that is dying becomes dominant. The number of living bacteria declines sharply over time in what is called the death or decline phase.
Source: http://www.enotes.com/bacteria-growth-reproduction-reference/bacteria-growth-reproduction

Question 12

What is the correct order of events for the growth and reproduction of bacteria?

A) Low growth phase – log phase – stationary phase - death phase
B) Lag phase – maximum phase - plateau phase – dominant phase
C) Lag phase – logarithmic phase – stationary phase - decline phase
D) Lag phase – doubling phase – stationary phase – deterioration phase

Question 13

Initial growth will take the most time if

A) Bacteria are healthy and adapting
B) Bacteria are damaged and thawing
C) Bacteria are frozen and weak
D) Bacteria are foreign and settling

Question 14

Which of the following statements is correct?

A) Oxygen is required for exponential bacterial growth
B) pH changes do not affect bacterial growth
C) Warming the conditions will extend the growth phase
D) Metabolism rates decline as toxic waste builds

Questions 15 - 18

The graph shows for different ages, the proportion of people in Australia who have a non-school qualification.

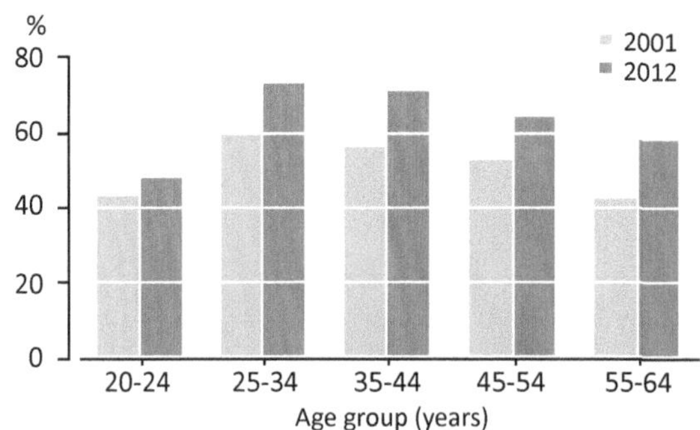

Source: http://www.abs.gov.au/ausstats/abs@.nsf/Products/6227.0~May+2012~Main+Features~Attainment?OpenDocument

Question 15

Suppose that there were 4 000 000 people aged 35 – 44 in 2001. How many of these people had a non-school qualification?

A) 2 000 000
B) 2 400 000
C) 2 200 000
D) 2 300 000

Question 16

In 2012 the average proportion of people with a non-school qualification

A) Were aged between 35 – 44-years-old
B) Was between 58% -78%
C) Were older than 34-years-old
D) Cannot be determined from just the information provided

Question 17

Which of the following is best supported by the information in the graph?

A) As people get older they increasingly obtain non-school qualifications
B) Between 2001 and 2012 a higher proportion of people at all ages obtained non-school qualifications
C) Between 2001 and 2012 more people at all ages obtained non-school qualifications
D) The number of people obtaining a non-school qualification increases at a decreasing rate

Question 18

Which of the following is best supported by the information in the graph?

A) Within 15 years of leaving school most people obtain a non-school qualification
B) Over time people have realised that they can obtain a higher income if they have a non-school qualification
C) People in their early 20s realise that a non-school qualification is necessary
D) Most 28-year-olds are studying

Questions 19 - 21

It is estimated that between 13 and 20 percent of all service personnel deployed to Iraq and Afghanistan since 2001, have or will develop post-traumatic stress disorder (PTSD). Depression is also common amongst ex-service personnel. Counselling can have some effect on addressing the symptoms that include anxiety, nightmares and increased levels of substance abuse. However, counselling is reported by ex-service personnel to be quite ineffective. An alternative for PTSD patients is the use of 'service dogs'. These dogs are specifically trained to assist PTSD patients to recover. They do so by waking patients who are having nightmares and staying with them as they calm and settle. Whilst there have been no double-blind, randomised controlled trials on the benefits of a service dog for PTSD patients there is much emerging anecdotal evidence from ex-service personnel on the benefit of trained dogs in assisting them to manage the effects of PTSD. It is thought that there are neurobiological effects of interacting with an animal; research has shown that when focus is on petting and playing with a dog, it can increase oxytocin and regulate serotonin levels. Oxytocin is a brain chemical that increases trust and calms the brain's fear response. Serotonin helps to overcome depression and anxiety.

Question 19

Which of the following is best supported by the information provided?

A) Post-traumatic stress disorder causes depression in ex-service personnel
B) The use of service dogs needs to be scientifically tested
C) Counselling is of little effectiveness to war veterans
D) Ex-service personnel should be routinely given serotonin

Question 20

From the text it can be concluded that animals

A) are beneficial for ex-service men and women
B) need to be cuddled for oxytocin to be released in the brain
C) can distract and assist a person suffering from depression
D) with PTSD can benefit from human touch

Question 21

A double-blind randomised control trial would

A) Mean that neither the experimenter nor the subject would know the essential details of the experiment was being conducted
B) Increase the chances of experimenter bias
C) Improve the chances of a successful clinical study as the dogs would be trained in secret
D) Increase the efficacy of any placebo being used

Questions 22-23

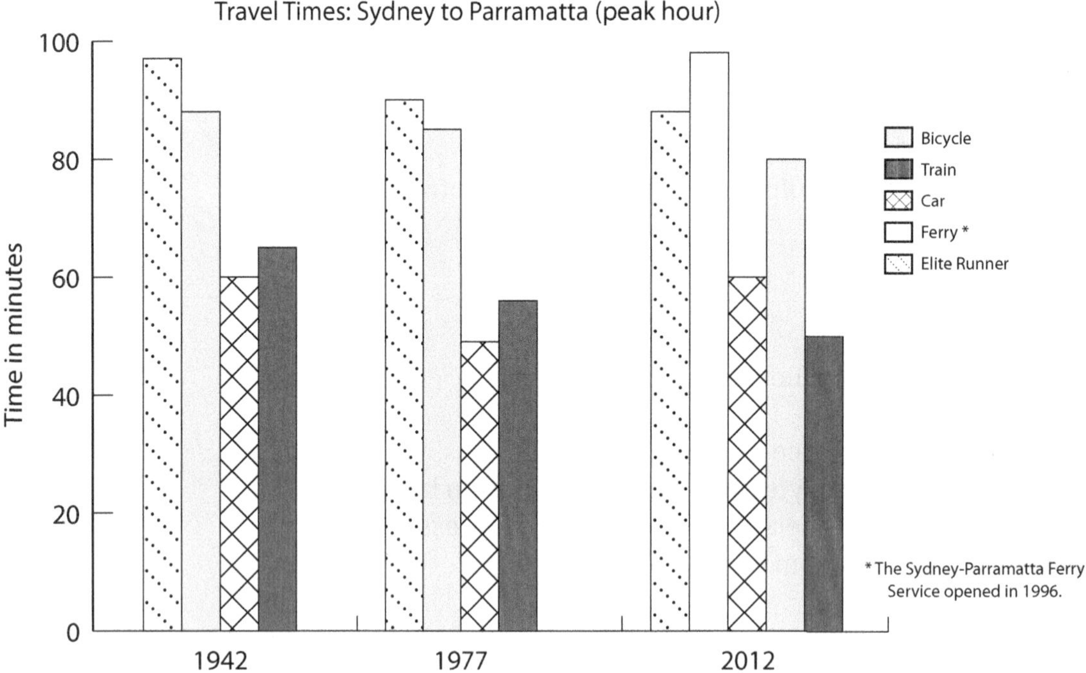

Question 22

Which of the following is best supported by the information?

A) All forms of transportation have become more efficient over time
B) Training methods for elite runners have improved
C) Bicycles are now made of lighter materials
D) A person catching the train in Sydney at 5.35pm should arrive in Parramatta before 6.30pm

Question 23

Which of the following does *NOT* account for the variation in car times?

A) The number of cars on the road has increased faster than the improvements to the road
B) There has been a change in the length of time it takes traffic signals to change
C) Transportation developments have caused road closures slowing motor vehicle times
D) There has been an increase in the number of speed cameras between 1977 and 2012

Question 24

Daniel noticed that he stirred sugar into tea by rotating the spoon clockwise. He then asked Jessica what she did and her reply was, "I'm left-handed so I stir it clockwise". In response to Jessica's reply Daniel asked 50 people to respond to a survey about which direction they rotate the spoon when stirring sugar into a hot drink. The responses are summarised in the Table.

Handedness	Stir clockwise	Stir counter-clockwise
Right-handed	29	12
Left-handed	8	1

Of the following which can be reliably concluded from the results shown?

A) Proportionally more right-handed people stir counter-clockwise than left-handed people stir clockwise
B) 74% of people stir clockwise
C) Left-handed people prefer to stir clockwise – Jessica was probably correct
D) It is uncommon for people to stir counter-clockwise

Questions 25 - 26

Querby and Felicity are potential candidates for the Blue Party for a general election to be held in Herath. Each party can field only one candidate. To be nominated as the successful candidate the nominee must be preferred on the basis of:

> Receiving a majority of votes from the party's three wings: youth wing, the women's wing and the men's wing. Each wing has 50 voting members
> Being preferred by at least two of the party wings

Question 25

Querby receives from 52 to 75 votes in total. To be the nominee, Querby must receive

A) 50 votes in youth wing, up to 25 votes in women's wing and no votes in the men's wing
B) An equal number of votes in any two wings and no votes in the remaining wing
C) An equal number of votes in any two wings and exactly half that number in the remaining wing
D) An equal number of votes in each of the wings

Question 26

If Querby wins 80 votes he must

A) Win at least two party wings
B) Win all three party wings
C) Win the election
D) Win at least one party wing

Questions 27 - 28

Sleep apnoea is a common sleep disorder characterised by abnormal breathing pauses occurring during sleep. The breathing pauses ('apnoea') can last for between ten seconds and a few minutes and can occur up to thirty times per hour of sleep. Hypopnoea occurs when respiratory rates are low for over ten seconds duration. It is common for normal breathing to return with a loud snort or choking sound. There are different types of sleep apnoea:

Obstructive (OSA): about 84% of sufferers
Central (CSA): about 0.5% of sufferers
Mixed (MSA): about 15.5% of sufferers

Sleep apnoea is diagnosed through a polysomnography. A polysomnography, or comprehensive 'sleep test', involves the placement of electrodes on the head and face, legs and finger. A further series of bands are placed around the chest and abdomen. The sensors are required so that the following tests can be conducted:

Electro-encephalography (EEG) – monitors brain waves
Electromyography (EMG) – monitors muscle tone
Electrocardiography (ECG) – this monitors the heart
Thoracoabdominal activity - records movements in chest and abdomen
Oronasal airflow - records airflow in mouth and nose
Pulse oximetry – measures heart rate and blood oxygen levels
Sound and video recording to record breathing and snoring and movements andbehaviour during the night

<u>Apnoea-hypopnoea index (AHI)</u>

The severity of OSA is determined by how many episodes of apnoea and hypopnoea, on average, are experienced over the course of an hour as measured by the apnoea-hypopnoea index (AHI):

Mild – an AHI reading of 5 to 20 episodes an hour
Moderate – an AHI reading of 21 to 50 episodes an hour
Severe – an AHI reading of more than 50 episodes an hour

An AHI reading of less than 10 is unlikely to be linked to a sleeping disorder.

Question 27

From the information the placement of an electrode on the finger is for measuring

A) Electro-encephalography
B) Pulse oximetry
C) Oronasal airflow
D) Thoracoabdominal activity

Question 28

A person experienced 300 apnoeas and 200 hypopnoeas over 480 minutes of sleep. The AHI would be:

A) 500 – extreme sleeping disorder
B) 62.5 - severe sleeping disorder
C) 20 – mild sleeping disorder
D) 1.2 – no sleeping disorder likely

Question 29

In a recent study on pain, anticipation and anxiety effects, a team of researchers stimulated a moderate level of pain by shining laser light onto the back of the hand of healthy participants. Some of these participants were then given a placebo in the form of a sham analgesic which they were told would reduce pain. The sham analgesic was a cream rubbed onto the back of the hand. To 'prove' the cream was effective researchers then shone reduced intensity laser onto the back of the hand.

Following this, both the control group and those given the sham placebo were subject to varying levels of laser intensity on the back of the hand intended to elicit moderate pain. Six weeks later the experiment was repeated. Researchers found that the placebo treatment was effective in reducing the perception of pain.

The results of this study suggest that

A) People's perception about medication affects the efficacy of the medication
B) Placebo treatments should be more widely utilised
C) Anticipation of pain increases anxiety and increases pain
D) Laser treatment can be moderately painful

Question 30

Genetic analysis and DNA testing can be used to determine paternity. A recent study of leaf cutter ants revealed that multiple paternity (polyandry) is possible. That is, genetic analysis revealed that two or more males in over ninety-three percent of colonies studied, contributed to the offspring. All offspring have some DNA that each of the parents have.

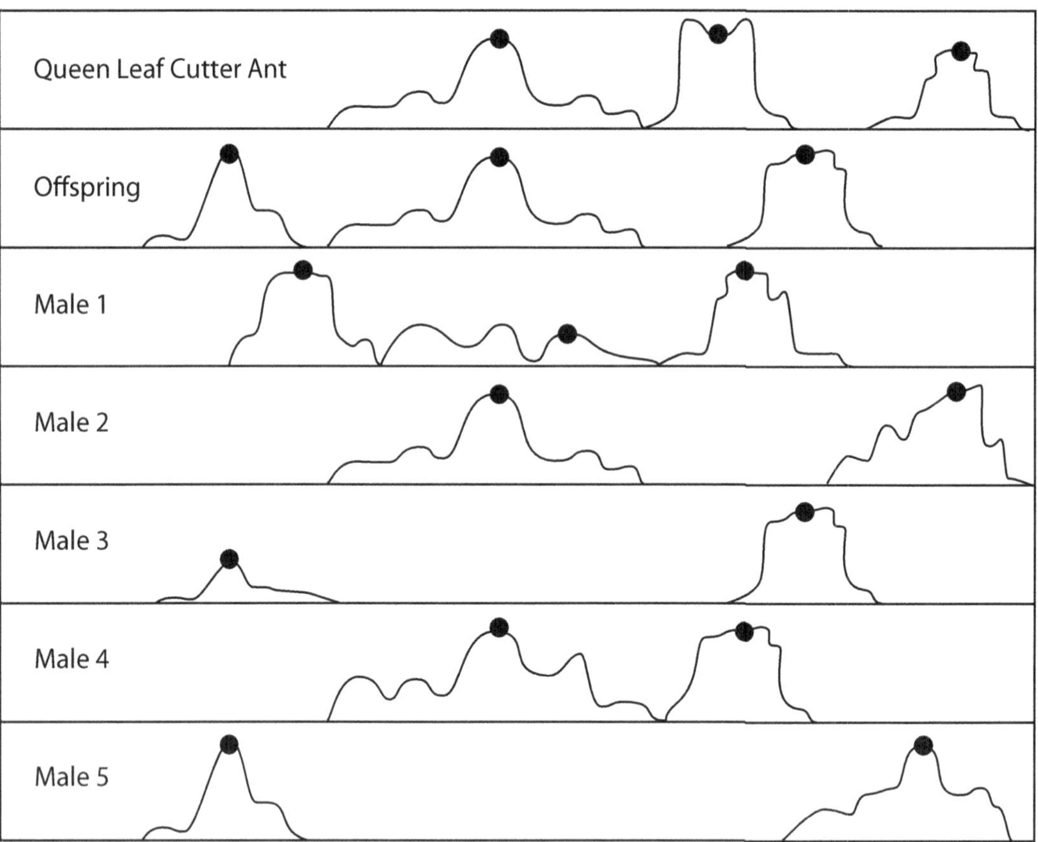

The fathers of the offspring are

A) Male 2 and Male 3
B) Male 2 and Male 4
C) Male 3 and Male 4
D) Male 3 and Male 5

Question 31

The following information refers to the ingredients in a product promoted as a health bar.

Nutrition information (average) **Servings per package: 4** **Average serving size – 28g (1 bar)**			
	Quantity per serving	**% daily intake per serving**	**Quantity per 100g**
Energy	490 kJ	6%	1750 kJ
Protein	2.1 g	4%	7.6 g
Fat, total **- saturated**	4.0g 2.1 g	6% 9%	14.4g 7.4 g
Carbohydrate **- sugars**	16.7 g 9.9 g	5% 11%	59.6 g 35.3 g
Dietary fibre	2.7 g	9%	9.6 g
Sodium	30 mg	1%	108 mg

What proportion of the average serve is sugars?

A) 5%
B) 11%
C) 35%
D) 16.7%

Questions 32 - 33

Recent university research appears to confirm that gaming improves creativity, decision-making and perception. The specific benefits are wide ranging, from improved hand-eye coordination in surgeons to vision changes that boost night driving ability. People who played action-based video and computer games made decisions 25% faster than others without sacrificing accuracy. The most adept gamers can make choices and act on them up to six times a second - four times faster than most people, researchers have found. Moreover, practiced game players can pay attention to more than six things at once without getting confused, compared with the four that someone can normally keep in mind, said University of Rochester researchers. The studies were conducted independently of the companies that sell video and computer games.

Scientists also found that women - who make up about 42% of computer and videogame players - were better able to mentally manipulate 3D objects, a skill at which men are generally more adept. Most studies looked at adults rather than children.

"Videogames change your brain," said University of Wisconsin psychologist C. Shawn Green, who studies how electronic games affect abilities. So does learning to read, playing the piano, or navigating the streets of London, which have all been shown to change the brain's physical structure. The powerful combination of concentration and rewarding surges of neurotransmitters like dopamine strengthen neural circuits in much the same way that exercise builds muscles. But "games definitely hit the reward system in a way that not all activities do," he said.

Adapted from: http://online.wsj.com/article/SB10001424052970203458604577263273943183932.html

Question 32

Which one of the following is supported by the information?

A) Video game playing increases hand-eye coordination
B) People who regularly play video games can multi-task more easily than those who do not
C) 42% of women were able to mentally manipulate three-dimensional objects after playing video games
D) Surgeons obtain improved sight from playing video games

Question 33

If it was shown that dopamine is released during the playing of violent video games then it could be concluded that

A) Violent video games will increase violent behaviour
B) Neural circuits that default to violent reactions will be strengthened
C) The brain's structure will change to accommodate violence without feeling fear
D) Game players will feel rewarded when playing violent games

Questions 34 - 36

Data for 11-year-olds – 17-year-olds watching on-line videos	
Over 20 hours per month	45%
Between 9 – 19 hours per month	32%
Less than 9 hours per month	23%
Data for 18-year-olds – 24-year-olds watching on-line videos	
Over 20 hours per month	48%
Between 9 – 19 hours per month	34%
Less than 9 hours per month	18%
Data for 25-year-olds – 31-year olds watching on-line videos	
Over 20 hours per month	42%
Between 9 – 19 hours per month	29%
Less than 9 hours per month	29%
Data for 32-year-olds – 38-year-olds watching on-line videos	
Over 20 hours per month	39%
Between 9 – 19 hours per month	23%
Less than 9 hours per month	38%
Data for 39-year-olds – 45-year-olds watching on-line videos	
Over 20 hours per month	24%
Between 9 – 19 hours per month	33%
Less than 9 hours per month	43%
Data for 46-year-olds – 52-year-olds watching on-line videos	
Over 20 hours per month	14%
Between 9 – 19 hours per month	17%
Less than 9 hours per month	69%
Data for 53-year-olds – 59-year-olds watching on-line videos	
Over 20 hours per month	12%
Between 9 – 19 hours per month	15%
Less than 9 hours per month	73%
Data for 60-year-olds – 66-year-olds watching on-line videos	
Over 20 hours per month	5%
Between 9 – 19 hours per month	12%
Less than 9 hours per month	83%

Question 34

According to this table,

A) As people get older they watch fewer videos on-line
B) The average 20-year-old watches four times as much on–line than the average fifty four-year-old
C) About half of those aged under twenty five years of age watch an average of two hours of on-line videos every three days
D) More people watch less than nine hours of on-line videos per month than watch more than nine hours per month

Question 35

Additional information:

Fact 1 Many older Australians watch educational and 'how to' videos on-line

Fact 2 Many younger Australians watch You Tube videos for entertainment

Fact 3 Ease of access and anonymity encourages people using the internet to download movies and file share

From this it can reasonably be concluded that

A) Australians aged over thirty nine years of age watch on-line videos for educational purposes
B) A person may use anonymity as a reason for downloading videos without paying for them
C) Australians aged under thirty years use the internet for entertainment
D) Older Australians are comfortable learning on-line

Questions 36 - 37

The following graphs refer to the same time period.

Population growth, quarterly

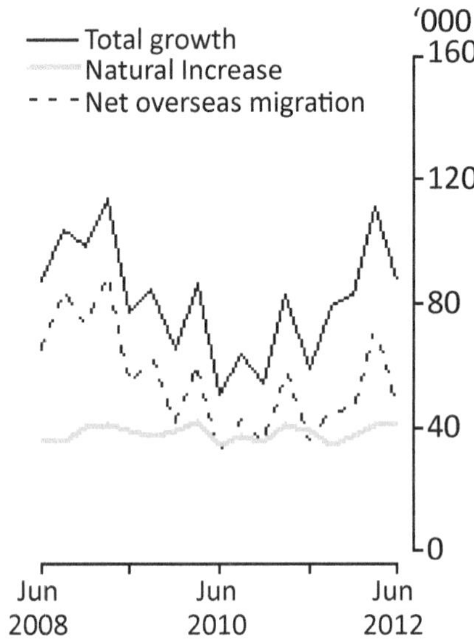

Population Growth Rate

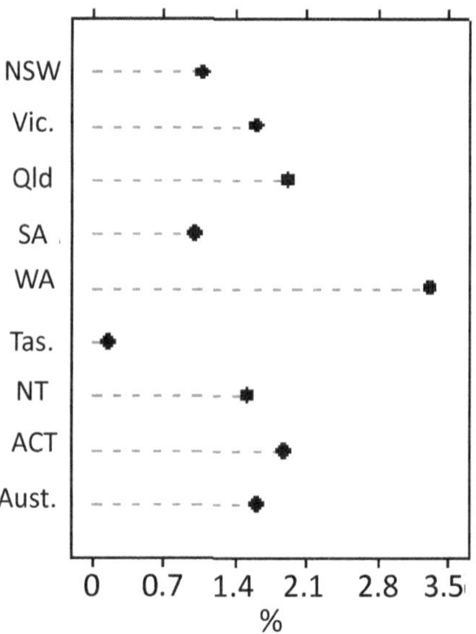

Question 36

From the information provided it follows that

A) Western Australia has the highest number of births
B) Proportionally, more migrants go to Western Australia than any other state
C) Birth rates rise when migration rates fall
D) Every six months migration rates spike higher

Question 37

From the information provided it follows that

A) The population increase for the year ended June 2012 was about 1 000 000
B) The population increase for the year ended June 2012 was about 90 000
C) The birth rate is constant but the migration rate fluctuates between 38 000 and 110 000 per year
D) The global economic crisis of 2008 – 2010 did not affect birth rates but did affect migration rates

Question 38

Over time athletes have sought to break the 4-minute time barrier for running a mile (1600 metres). The 4-minute barrier was first broken by Roger Bannister in 1954. The graph below records various mile world records over time. The current record was set in 1999 by Moroccan runner Hicham El Guerrouj and has not been beaten since then.

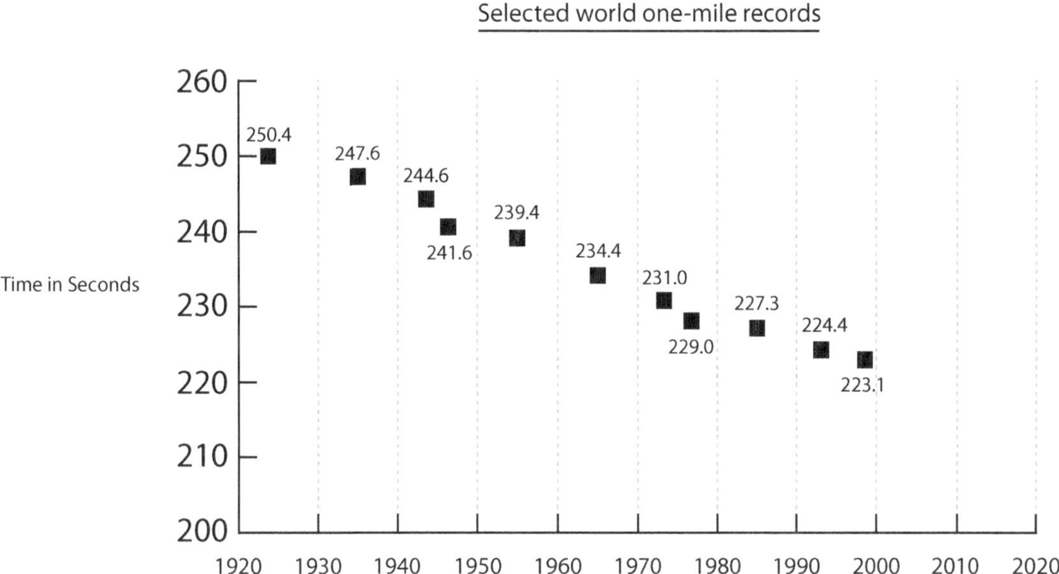

Which of the following can be reliably concluded from the results shown?

A) The next world record time should be 222.1 seconds
B) The largest fall in record times was 3 seconds
C) On average records are broken every 7.1 years
D) On average the speed improved by 0.36 seconds per year

Questions 39 - 40

It is common for transportation authorities to release data on braking distances for vehicles at various speeds. The total stopping distance of a vehicle is made up of four different components: the driver's perception time, the driver's reaction time, the vehicle's reaction time and the vehicle's braking capacity.

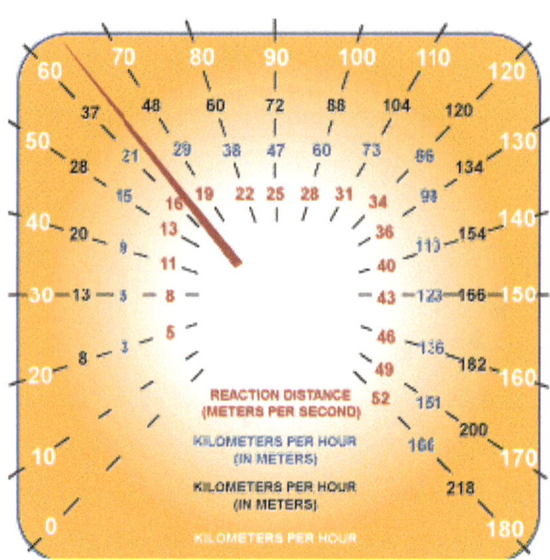

Question 39

From the information above it follows that

A) Reaction distance = Driver's perception time + (driver + vehicle) reaction time
B) Reaction distance = Driver's reaction time + vehicle's reaction time
C) Stopping distance = Reaction distance + vehicle's braking capacity
D) Stopping distance = Speed x time

Question 40

At a speed of 52 kilometres per hour the stopping distance would be

A) 180 metres
B) 93 metres
C) 72 metres
D) 31 metres

Questions 41 and 42

There are four different types of muscle cramps, distinguished by their cause and the muscle groups affected. The types of muscle cramps are:

Genuine or 'true' cramps
Cramps caused by tetany
Contracture cramps
Dystonic cramps

Genuine or 'true' cramps

These cramps are the most common form of cramps and are caused by hyperexcitability of the nerves that stimulate the muscles. These cramps can occur from fatigue arising from vigorous activity, as a protective mechanism following injury to a muscle, excessive fluid loss (including dehydration), hyperventilation, sodium depletion, low levels of calcium, potassium or magnesium in body fluids. Vitamin D deficiency can contribute indirectly to genuine cramps as low levels of vitamin D contribute to poor absorption of calcium.

Cramps caused by tetany

In tetany, all of the nerve cells in the body are activated, which then stimulate the muscles. This reaction causes spasms or cramps throughout the body. Low calcium and low magnesium levels, which increase the activity of nerve tissue nonspecifically, also can also cause tetanic cramps.

Contractures

Contractures are relatively rare and result when the muscles are unable to relax. A loss of adenosine triphosphate (ATP) prevents muscles from being able to relax and thus they spasm. ATP is an energy chemical within the cell.

Dystonic cramps

Dystonic cramps occur when the muscles that are not needed for the intended movement are stimulated to contract. They arise from a neurological disorder. Dystonic cramps occur in muscles that work in the opposite direction of the intended movement, or that amplify the movement. They tend to occur in the face, neck, hand, jaw and muscles around the eyes. An example of dystonic cramps is "writer's cramp".

Whilst it is commonly thought that cramps are caused by a lack of minerals lost in sweat this is now not considered generally true. Thus, the use of salt is not the remedy for most cramping, particularly for genuine cramps. Simply stretching a cramping muscle is more likely to be most effective.

Question 41

Which one of the following is most strongly supported by the information?

A) Sportspeople must replenish fluids regularly during vigorous exercise to prevent cramping
B) Vitamin D deficiency can cause genuine cramps and cramps caused by tetany
C) Cramps in the hands are dystonic and occur when typing
D) Both hyperexcitability and relaxation can be the source of cramping

Question 42

From the information it can be concluded that

A) Further research needs to be done on the cause of genuine cramps for appropriate remedies to be found
B) Cramps are natural and need to be managed as a part of everyday living
C) Drinks with sodium, potassium, adenosine phosphate, calcium and magnesium should help manage cramps
D) Stretching the hands during writer's cramp should be effective for relief

Question 43

A family needs to escape from a burning apartment through a partially blocked stairwell. The power to the building has been cut and the stairwell is extremely dark and dangerous. The family has access to a torch and the only way through the stairwell is through using the torch. The father can make it in out of the building in 1 minute, the mother in 2 minutes, the older daughter in 4 and the youngest son in 5 minutes. However, only two persons can go through the stairwell at one time, moving at the speed of the slower one.

There is 12 minutes for the whole family to escape from the apartment fire and get safely to the ground. After this the stairwell will collapse.

From the information it can be concluded that

A) At least one of the family members will be trapped in the building
B) The first people to leave the building must be the parents
C) Exactly one family member will be trapped in the building
D) The parents should leave the building first and last

Questions 44 and 45

Curing is a process that involves controlling the rate and extent of moisture loss from concrete during cement hydration. It may be either after it has been placed into position or during the manufacture of concrete products thereby providing time for hydration to occur. Since the hydration of cement does take time – days, and even weeks rather than hours – curing must be undertaken for a reasonable period of time if the concrete is to achieve its potential strength and durability. Curing may also encompass the control of temperature since this affects the rate at which cement hydrates. Curing is designed primarily to keep the concrete moist, by preventing the loss of moisture during the period in which it is gaining its strength. Curing may be applied in a number of ways and the most appropriate means of curing may be dictated by the site or the construction method. Curing by preventing excessive loss of moisture from the concrete either by:

Leaving the formwork in place
Covering the concrete with an impermeable membrane after the formwork has been removed
By application of a suitable chemical curing agent (wax etc)
Or by a combination of such methods

Or through:

Curing by continuously wetting the exposed surface thereby preventing the loss of moisture from it. Ponding or spraying the surface with water are methods typically employed to this end

Adapted from: http://www.concrete.net.au/publications/pdf/Curing06.pdf

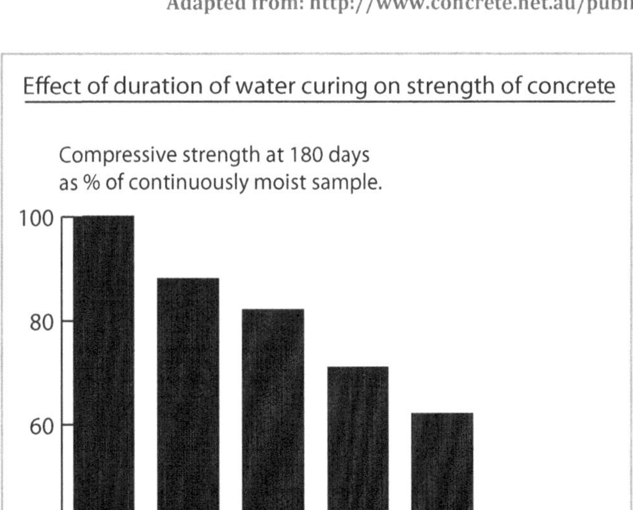

Question 44

From the information it follows that

A) When concrete dries in air it is 40% of its full strength at 180 days
B) Wax acts as a porous membrane allowing water into the concrete but not out
C) At 180 days concrete reaches its maximum strength
D) Curing for 360 days would make concrete stronger than curing for 180 days

Question 45

Which of the following can be reliably concluded from the information provided?

A) In earthquake-prone areas concrete should be cured for at least 14 days
B) The effectiveness of curing is evident within 3 days as it leads to 63% more concrete strength
C) Concrete doubles its strength if cured for 180 days instead of 3 days
D) After 4 weeks of curing the increase in strength gained by an additional 18 weeks of curing is marginal

Question 46

The caesarean section rate has shown an upward trend over the past 10 years, increasing from 23.3% nationally in 2000 to a peak of 31.5% in 2009. There were 59,051 caesarean sections performed in 2000 and 92,687 caesarean sections performed in 2009.Among all women who gave birth in 2009, 18.4% had a caesarean section without labour and 13.0% had a caesarean section with labour. The proportion of caesarean section deliveries varies between states and territories; ranging from 27.9% in the Australian Capital Territory to 33.3% in both Queensland and Western Australia. Caesarean section rates varied by maternal age - from 17.5% for mothers younger than 20 to 47.2% for mothers aged 40 and over, and by hospital sector - 42.5% for women in private hospitals and 28.4% for those in public hospitals. Repeat caesarean sections occurred for 83.6% of mothers who had previously had a caesarean section.

In 2009:

> More babies were born in October than in any other month
> More male babies were born than female (51.4% male, 48.6% female)
> 75% of women who went into labour had painkilling drugs administered
> Over 8% of babies were born preterm (before 37 completed weeks gestation). The average duration of pregnancy was 38.8 weeks
> 1.6% of all mothers had a multiple delivery (twins or more). Multiple deliveries increase with advancing maternal age, peaking in women aged 35–39 years.

Source: http://www.aihw.gov.au/access/201204/feature/mums-and-bubs.cfm

From the information it follows that

A) About one-sixth of male babies were born by caesarean birth
B) Rich women are more likely to have caesarean births than middle-income women
C) Women who do not labour during birth outnumber those who do labour during birth
D) Older women have more caesarean births as twins are born through this method

Question 47

A survey of 22,000 mothers in Queensland purports to explode the "myth" that women opt for a C-section to avoid the rigours of natural childbirth, or out of convenience. Rather than being "too posh to push", most women having a caesarean were acting on the advice of their doctor, often without understanding the full ramifications of the surgery. Only 52 per cent of those who elected to have a C-section made the decision in an informed way, the survey by the University of Queensland's Centre for Mothers and Babies found. In the case of women who underwent the procedure in unplanned or emergency circumstances, informed decision-making dropped to 20 per cent. Over all, the caesarean rate has increased by 74 per cent in Australia over the past 20 years and in Queensland, where it is highest, C-sections account for a third of all births. Just on 48 per cent of babies delivered in private hospitals in Queensland are by caesarean section, against 27.8 per cent for public hospitals.

"When it comes to caesarean sections, our research shows the increase seems to be largely driven by the recommendations of doctors, particularly in private hospitals," QCMB director Sue Kruske said. "This would indicate the notion that women are choosing to have a caesarean because they are 'too posh to push' is incorrect."

Royal Australian and New Zealand College of Obstetricians and Gynaecologists president Rupert Sherwood agreed the "too posh to push" argument was overblown. In his experience, fewer than 5 per cent of C-sections were performed on women with no medical indications for the surgery. Dr Sherwood attributed the rising caesarean rate to factors such as women having children later and increased obesity - both of which compounded the risk of natural delivery - and to wider choices in how to give birth.

http://www.theaustralian.com.au/news/health-science/doctors-advice-the-reason-for-soaring-rates-of-c-sections/story-e6frg8y6-1226247810762

According to the information provided it can be reasonably concluded that

A) Caesarean rates are increasing because women do not want to face the pain of natural childbirth
B) Doctors need to be educated about the impact of their advice on patients
C) Improved understanding of the nature of caesarean would reduce the incidence of it
D) Risks associated with natural births are on the rise

Question 48

Australia has the highest reported prevalence of food allergy in the world. This was a key issue addressed at the annual scientific meeting of the Australasian Society of Child Immunology. Professor Johan Garssen of the Danone Research Centre for Specialised Nutrition and Utrecht University Department Immunopharmacology of the Netherlands, presented the latest research on possible ways to manage the problem of food allergies, which was a global phenomenon - although Australians appeared to be the most prevalent sufferers.
The prevalence of allergic diseases and asthma has increased dramatically over the past few decades, affecting an estimated 20% of the population in developed countries, especially children. The most dramatic increase in food allergy, earlier presentation and increasing persistence of disease was cows' milk protein allergy with an estimated prevalence of 3% in the paediatric population. Although the rates of allergic diseases in other regions of Asia are reported to be lower than in Australia, the rates of eczema, asthma and allergic rhinitis have already risen rapidly. Moreover, the Asian populations have been reported to be more susceptible to allergic disease in response to Western style environmental changes, as supported by evidence from immigration studies. Professor Garssen considered a number of different hypotheses postulated to explain the increase in prevalence of allergic diseases in Australia and elsewhere. These were said to include a failure of immune tolerance, and environmental factors, such as microbial exposure ("hygiene hypothesis"), infections, diet and air pollution, both during pre-natal as well as during postnatal development. Several epidemiological studies support the hygiene hypothesis and have clearly shown that modifications of the pattern of microbial exposure and colonisation represent a critical factor underlying the rise in prevalence of atopic disorders. Professor Garssen said an important group of immune-modulating compounds in human milk are non-digestible human milk oligosaccharides (HMOS). HMOS are known for their ability to selectively stimulate the growth and activity of bacteria that exert positive health effects. They have been described to promote the development of a tolerogenic environment in the gut, thereby reducing the risk of inappropriate immune responses like food allergy.

Adapted from: http://www.ausfoodnews.com.au/2012/09/10/australia-has-highest-rate-of-food-allergy-sufferers-more-research-needed.html

According to the information, which of the following statements are True and which are False?

I Increased cleanliness is linked with higher allergy rates

II Cow's milk protein is not beneficial to young children

III Breast-feeding reduces allergy responses

A) II and III are true
B) I and II are false but III is true
C) I and III are true
D) I, II are true but III is false

ANSWERS

Summary & Worked Solutions
Multiple Choice Answer Sheet

Summary of Answers

Question 1	C	Question 13	B	Question 25	B	Question 37	A
Question 2	B	Question 14	A	Question 26	D	Question 38	D
Question 3	C	Question 15	D	Question 27	B	Question 39	A
Question 4	A	Question 16	D	Question 28	B	Question 40	D
Question 5	D	Question 17	B	Question 29	A	Question 41	B
Question 6	B	Question 18	A	Question 30	D	Question 42	D
Question 7	D	Question 19	B	Question 31	C	Question 43	D
Question 8	A	Question 20	C	Question 32	A	Question 44	A
Question 9	C	Question 21	A	Question 33	D	Question 45	D
Question 10	A	Question 22	D	Question 34	C	Question 46	A
Question 11	D	Question 23	B	Question 35	B	Question 47	C
Question 12	C	Question 24	C	Question 36	B	Question 48	C

Answers with fully worked solutions

Question 1

C

The Bob Tail Blue-tongue is not specifically mentioned in the article. However, it is quite clear from the text that young are born between December and April – that is December – February which are the summer months in the Southern Hemisphere.

Question 2

B

This requires estimation as 16km is not specifically listed as a distance. However, predicted 5km and 10km times are listed.

The sum of these times for a VO_2 max of 89.9 is 37:59. Thus 16km would be well under 48 minutes.
The sum of these times for a VO_2 max of 79.1 is 44:21. Thus 16km would be very close to 48 minutes.
The sum of these times for a VO_2 max of 82.7 is 42:07. Thus 16km would be under 48 minutes.
The sum of these times for a VO_2 max of 75.5 is 46:43. Thus, 16km would be well over 48 minutes.

Hence B is correct.

Question 3

C

In the population 50% are girls or 1,000 children. There are also 1,000 boys. As 25% of girls play netball then 250 girls play netball. As 20% of boys play cricket then 200 boys play cricket. This means that 450 children play sport. 25% of all of the children get private tuition. This is 500 children in total (25% of 2,000). If 300 of the students play sport and also get tutoring then it follows that:

150 only play a sport and do not get tutoring. 500 children do tutoring (300 of these also play a sport) and 150 play a sport thus 650 students have some form of activity. Thus 1,350 do no activities, hence C is correct.

Question 4

A

The number of employed persons rose from 11,529,400 to 11,535,200. The number of unemployed person also increased, in this case from 647,800 to 648,500. It does not follow that because unemployment rose between October and November that it must also rise to December.

Question 5

D

Tricky question! If the large glasses are C and D then water will spill – one eighth of a glass. This is shown as follows:

B poured into C means C is now three quarters full and C is empty. A poured into D means D is three quarters full and A is empty. Half of D being poured into A means that A (a small glass) is now three quarters full and D is three eighths full. If C is now poured into D then three quarters of a full glass is being poured into a glass three eighths full, leading to an overflow of one eighth. Thus A and C are wrong.

If the small glasses are A and C then when B is poured into C a quarter of a glass of water overflows from C and C remains full. Thus B is eliminated.

If the large glasses are A and D then when B is poured into C (small glass into small glass) B is empty and C is full. When A is poured into D then A is empty (large glass) and D is full. If half of D is poured into A then both are half full as at the start. If all of C is poured into D then D is full and C is empty with no water spilling – thus option D is correct.

Question 6

B

X = 300 – (29 + 33 + 35 + 24 + 42 + 131) = 300 – 294 = 6

Y = 100 – (2 + 10 + 11 + 11 + 8 + 14) = 100 – 56 = 44%

Hence B is correct.

Question 7

D

Safety is a significant factor affecting motor vehicle purchases specifically but not consumer purchases generally. Thus A is incorrect as a conclusion. Cost is twice as important as reliability as the most important factor affecting car buyers but on other measures it may not be. Power is insignificant in the context of what is most sought and is significant in what is least important thus D is correct.

Question 8

A

The text states that 95% of Australian children are receiving the three doses of the vaccine within their first 6 months of life, thus it is clear that by 18 months most children in Australia are fully vaccinated for whooping cough.

Since not all complications of whooping cough lead to brain damage (it would be an assumption – brain damage is a *possible* complication) then B is incorrect. The generalised statement of C cannot be drawn from the information given and therefore it can be ruled out. D may be factually correct but there is nothing in the information to indicate whether this is the case or not and therefore it must be treated as not true.

Question 9

C

A is not supported by the information given. Indeed the opposite is probably true. The statement in B is too general and cannot be supported from the information which is specific to the pertussis vaccine. D is not relevant. The statement that 'because of its side effects the whole cell vaccine was abandoned' leads the thinking that acellular pertussis vaccine must have fewer side effects and hence C is correct.

Question 10

A

The article indicates that A is true. It is not clear whether, as a general rule, whole cell vaccines are more effective that acellular vaccines, though it may be the case with respect to whooping cough and the pertussis vaccine. It is also unclear whether the mutation of the bacteria is causing the lack of effectiveness. D is clearly untrue as rates are increasing despite high levels of vaccination.

Question 11

D

Assume the old man is telling the truth. If so then he loves Italian coffee. The younger man must therefore be lying since 'at least one is lying'. Thus he too loves Italian coffee. However, this is not true as one man loves Italian coffee and the other loves Vietnamese coffee. Hence A is incorrect. Assume the old man is lying. This means he loves Vietnamese coffee. If this is the case then the younger man must love Italian coffee and thus he too must be lying hence D holds. If the young man is telling the truth then he loves Vietnamese coffee. This must mean that the old man is lying and he too loves Vietnamese coffee. However, we know they both love different coffee, hence the young man must be lying.

Thus D is correct

Question 12

C

Lag phase (line 6) – Logarithmic phase (line 11) – Stationary phase (line 20) – Decline phase (last line).

Question 13

B

From the stimulus:

The lag phase may be short or long the latter occurs if the bacteria are damaged or recovering from deep-freeze storage. Thus B is correct.

Question 14

A

The explosive growth of bacteria slows as oxygen becomes depleted and as the nutrient levels decline. pH changes are also significant. Hence B is incorrect. Warmth tends to increase growth rates and thus will shorten the growth phase. Metabolism rates decline for a number of reasons but it is not suggested that toxic waste levels are a cause. Thus A is correct.

Question 15

D

This requires careful estimation. The proportion of people in the 35-44 years age group who had a non-school qualification was close to 57%. Thus A is too low, and B is too high. Of the remaining options C represents 56 % and D represents 57.5%.

D is therefore most correct.

Question 16

D

Since the number of people within each age category is unknown there can be no certainty with any of options A B and C. Hence D is correct.

Question 17

B

A is incorrect as the proportions decline with time. Since it is unclear what the population is then C cannot be certain. Again with D the number of people in each age bracket is not known hence there can be no certainty about this statement. It is clear however that at all ages a greater proportion of people obtained no-school qualifications. The higher columns for 2012 indicate this.

Thus B is correct.

Question 18

A

It is not clear the relationship between non-school qualifications and income thus B cannot be certain. It is similarly not clear that there is a realisation that non-school qualifications is necessary even though there is a spike in the 25-34 age bracket. There is not enough information to confidently state the situation for 28-year-olds, however there is enough information supported by the graph that indicates most people after up to about age 35 do get a non-school qualification (this would include university course, TAFE course or similar).

Question 19

B

The relationship between PTSD and depression is not discussed thus A is not supported by the information even though there may be some relationship between the two. Counselling can have some effect on the symptoms but it is reported that ex-service personnel say it is quite ineffective. It is however not a general rule and hence C must be eliminated. As not all ex-service personnel are subject to symptoms of PTSD or depression the routine taking of serotonin is unwarranted. Even if all ex-service personnel were subject to the symptoms the taking of serotonin could not be routine practice.

B is supported as there is some conjecture as to whether the dogs are effective for ex-service personnel. However, rather than use anecdotes proper scientific tested should be done.

Thus B is correct.

Question 20

C

It is not clear that any or all animals are beneficial for ex-service men and women thus A does not hold. It is also not clear whether an animal must be cuddled for the release of oxytocin in the brain, thus B is incorrect. The text deals with the effect of dogs on ex-service personnel not the other way around, thus D is incorrect.

What is clear is that animals can distract a person and thus assist ex-service personnel suffering from the effects of war, such as depression. Thus C is correct.

Question 21

A

To answer this a candidate needs to understand what a double blind control trial is. Such a trial requires that the subject cannot know the crucial details of the experiment as this could affect their behaviour. Similarly, for it to be 'double blind' the experimenter cannot know the essential details of the experiment.

The idea is to minimise possible bias and thus get results that are not affected by expectation.

Question 22

D

The information indicates that times have fallen for all modes of transportation and for runners. However, there is nothing in the information that indicates why the times have generally fallen.

Thus A is not supported by the information and nor is B or C. According to the graph it takes 55 minutes to get from Sydney to Parramatta by train. This means a person leaving Sydney at 5.35pm should get to Parramatta 55 minutes later at 6.30PM thus D is correct and is supported by the information.

Question 23

B

Each of A, C and D would explain the variation in car times and are plausible in a growing city. However, what is certain is that we cannot know whether the length of time changes in traffic signals has shortened or lengthened and hence we cannot be certain of the effect of this.

Question 24

C

12 out of 41 people who are right-handed stir counter-clockwise. This equates to about 28% whereas 8 out of 9 people who are left-handed stir clockwise. This equates to 88%. Thus A is incorrect.

37 (29 + 8) people out of 50 stir clockwise. This is equal to 74% of the sample, but the sample size is small and thus is cannot be reliable concluded as a generalisation, thus B is incorrect.

Even though only small proportion of the sample size stirred counter-clockwise, 26% of the sample is by no means 'uncommon'. Thus D is incorrect.

Even though the sample size is relatively small clear trends are emerging – one being that people generally prefer to stir clockwise. Hence C is true.

Question 25

B

We must assume that Querby received the lowest number of votes in the range given: 52 votes. Only 26 are required in any party wing and 52 can be divided into two lots of 26 – which would be a majority of the votes in any of the wings.

From this it follows that A is not correct, as 25 is not enough to be a majority in the second party wing. C is also not correct as it implies a division such as 24, 24 and 12 (60 votes) which is not enough to win any party wing. Finally, D is also not correct as even 75 votes or 25 in each of 3 wings is not enough to win the candidature.

Thus only B is correct.

Question 26

D

80 votes can be enough to win two party wings but need not be. Consider this: if a candidate wins 50 votes in one party wing and 15 in each of the other two then they have 80 votes but have not won two party wings. Thus A and B are not correct. Similarly, since 80 votes can mean only winning one party wing it follows that C is also not correct.

However, since 80 divided by three is 26, 27 and 27 (as close to one third as possible) any combination that reduces any one of these must increase at least one of the other two party wing votes thus D must be correct.

Question 27

B

The electro-encephalography monitors brain waves and hence the finger is not relevant, hence A is incorrect. The oronasal airflow records airflow in the mouth and nose and thus the finger is not relevant, hence C is incorrect. The thoracoabdominal activity records movements in the chest and abdomen and thus D is not correct either.

B is correct as the pulse can be measured in the fingers.

Question 28

B

300 apnoeas and 200 hypopnoeas equals 500 in the space of 480 minutes. 480 minutes equates to 8 hours. Thus 500   8 = an AHI of 62.5

B is correct.

Question 29

A

In the experiment people were told that the sham analgesic would reduce the pain they felt and this was "confirmed" when they felt the effects of reduced laser intensity. Psychologically they would relate the placebo as having a pain reducing effect.

Thus when the placebo was effective after 6 weeks the results suggest that perception about medication affects the effectiveness of the medication.

Question 30

D

The key here is to match the pattern within the DNA samples to that of the offspring. Note, however that this must be done separate from the DNA pattern of the mother as the offspring have DNA from all parents. Thus the DNA of the mother (Queen) must not be considered.

The matches are from Male 3 and Male 5 (look at the patterns closely).

Question 31

C

Tricky question! The question here is asking the proportion of sugars in the average serve not as a proportion of the average daily allowance. The answer is to look in the right hand column. Here it can be seen that per 100g about 35.5g is sugar. This must mean that the proportion in any serve is roughly 35% including an 'average' serve. Note, this is a 'health' bar!

Question 38

D

It is not possible to extrapolate future possible record times, thus A is incorrect. According to the graph the largest fall in times between the records listed was 5 seconds (1953 – 1965) thus B is not correct. The title of the graph is "selected" world one-mile records and shows 11 records in the period 1923 – 1999 – a period of 76 years. If this is averaged out, it would suggest there is a fall in record every 6.9 years. However, consider that the record has not fallen since 1999. If the time between 1999 and 2013 is considered then there is a case to be made that the time should be 90 years not 76 years. Therefore it cannot be reliably concluded that the record time is broken every 7 years. Hence C is incorrect.

The record fell from 250.4 seconds to 223.1 seconds in 76 years. This means a 27.3 second fall in the 76-year time period, or 0.36 seconds per year. Thus the speed 'improved' on average 0.36 seconds per year.

Question 39

A

The reaction distance must include the time it takes for the driver to perceive, otherwise the graph of stopping distances would be incorrect. Hence B must be incorrect. The stopping distance would be the sum of the reaction distance and the braking distance (not braking capacity – though it would be directly proportional to breaking capacity). Thus C is incorrect. The stopping distance may be calculated by multiplying average speed x time from the time the braking commenced to when the car stopped – thus D is too simplistic and is incorrect.

As the time to react includes the driver's perception time and the two reaction times (driver's reaction time and vehicle reaction time) then A is correct.

Question 40

D

There are four places on the graph where the number 52 appears. The outside white numbers refer to the speed of the vehicle in kilometres per hour. The second set of numbers going in from outside refers to the total stopping distance in metres. The third number is the braking distance and the inner number is the reaction distance. Thus the correct answer is slightly over 28 metres which is the stopping distance at 50kmph.

Question 41

B

The last paragraph states that cramps are now not thought to be caused by the lack of minerals lost in sweat. Further, it is not clear that all sportspeople sweat at rates that mean they will all lose fluids commensurate with fluid losses leading to cramping, nor is it clear how long the vigorous exercise needs to be prior to possible fluid replacement thus A cannot be correct. Cramps in the hand may be dystonic and can arise from repetitious activity (such as writing) but it cannot be reliably concluded that they are always dystonic, hence C can be ruled out. There is also nothing in the text to suggest that cramps are caused by relaxing (even though it is the common experience of people to experience cramps in the calves at night whilst sleeping) - thus D can be discounted.

Vitamin D deficiency is said to contribute directly to genuine cramps as 'low levels of vitamin D contribute to poor absorption of calcium'. Low calcium is also a cause of cramps caused by tetany, thus it follows that low levels of vitamin D can cause both types of cramps and B is correct.

Question 42

D

There seems to be plenty of understanding as to the cause of genuine cramps hence A is not supported by the information. There is nothing to suggest B, thus it is not correct. Whilst common belief is that mineralised drinks do help, appropriate levels of vitamin D would need to be present in the body for the uptake of minerals.

It does state that stretching a cramping muscle is likely to be most effective and thus D can be reliably concluded.

Question 43

D

First the parents - mother and father leave. This takes 2 minutes. The father then returns adding another minute. The time elapsed is 3 minutes. Next both children go to the mother. This takes 5 minutes - the time of the slowest child. The total elapsed time is now 8 minutes. The mother now returns to the father which takes another 2 minutes. The total elapsed time is now 10 minutes. Finally both parents now leave the building, taking 2 minutes to get out and reach their children (the time of the slower person). The total elapsed time is 12 minutes. Thus D - the parents leave first and last- is correct.

Question 44

A

Wax is non-porous and acts to hold in moisture thus B is not correct. It is not clear from the graph whether 180 days is the time it takes to meet maximum strength but there is a comparison to the strength at 180 days. Hence C cannot be considered correct. We cannot extrapolate beyond the graph as in D thus it is not correct.

The right hand column shows that concrete drying in air is 40% of its full strength at 180 days (left hand column) thus A is correct.

Question 45

D

There can be no reliable statement made in regards to earthquake-prone areas hence A cannot be reliably concluded. The curing process for 3 days leads to 23% greater strength than air drying alone and thus the 63% claim is not correct. Concrete becomes about 37% stronger if cured for 180 days, not doubling in strength thus C can be omitted. Lastly, 4 weeks equates to 28 days. At 28 days the concrete is about 95% as strong as it is at 180 days of curing, thus it can be reliably concluded that the additional 18 weeks of curing gives marginal increase in strength.

Question 46

A

It should not be assumed that only 'rich' women use private hospitals thus B is not correct. The reference to laboring during birth was specific to caesarean and cannot be generalised as it is in C thus C is not correct. The relationship between older women having caesarean and multiple births with advancing age should not imply that twins lead to caesarean section as a matter of course thus D can be omitted.

Given that about 31.5% of children are born through caesarean section and that on average the same number of males and females are born then it follows that about 16.7% (or half) of all male babies would be born by caesarean.

Question 47

C

The evidence is that caesarean is not on the increase on account of women not wanting to face pain but rather that women are acting on the advice of doctors and in so doing are not understanding the implications of the caesarean. It follows then that improved understanding of the effects of caesarean should lower the incidence hence C is correct. There is nothing in the text to directly conclude that A, B or D is a reasonable conclusion.

Question 48

C

It is clear that several studies support the hygiene hypothesis and thus I must be true. This means that B can be excluded. Whilst cow's milk protein is a source of allergy there is no indication from the information that it is not beneficial to young children and hence II must be false. This now excludes A and D. Since breast feeding increases the amount of HMOS which directly reduces the risk of immune responses then statement III is true and thus C is correct.

Essential Preparation for

UMAT

UNDERGRADUATE MEDICINE & HEALTH SCIENCES ADMISSION TEST

MULTIPLE CHOICE ANSWER SHEET

Use pencil when filling out this sheet

Fill in the circle correctly			
●	(B)	(C)	(D)

If you make a mistake neatly cross it out and circle the correct response			
⊗	●	(C)	(D)

1	(A)	(B)	(C)	(D)	25	(A)	(B)	(C)	(D)
2	(A)	(B)	(C)	(D)	26	(A)	(B)	(C)	(D)
3	(A)	(B)	(C)	(D)	27	(A)	(B)	(C)	(D)
4	(A)	(B)	(C)	(D)	28	(A)	(B)	(C)	(D)
5	(A)	(B)	(C)	(D)	29	(A)	(B)	(C)	(D)
6	(A)	(B)	(C)	(D)	30	(A)	(B)	(C)	(D)
7	(A)	(B)	(C)	(D)	31	(A)	(B)	(C)	(D)
8	(A)	(B)	(C)	(D)	32	(A)	(B)	(C)	(D)
9	(A)	(B)	(C)	(D)	33	(A)	(B)	(C)	(D)
10	(A)	(B)	(C)	(D)	34	(A)	(B)	(C)	(D)
11	(A)	(B)	(C)	(D)	35	(A)	(B)	(C)	(D)
12	(A)	(B)	(C)	(D)	36	(A)	(B)	(C)	(D)
13	(A)	(B)	(C)	(D)	37	(A)	(B)	(C)	(D)
14	(A)	(B)	(C)	(D)	38	(A)	(B)	(C)	(D)
15	(A)	(B)	(C)	(D)	39	(A)	(B)	(C)	(D)
16	(A)	(B)	(C)	(D)	40	(A)	(B)	(C)	(D)
17	(A)	(B)	(C)	(D)	41	(A)	(B)	(C)	(D)
18	(A)	(B)	(C)	(D)	42	(A)	(B)	(C)	(D)
19	(A)	(B)	(C)	(D)	43	(A)	(B)	(C)	(D)
20	(A)	(B)	(C)	(D)	44	(A)	(B)	(C)	(D)
21	(A)	(B)	(C)	(D)	45	(A)	(B)	(C)	(D)
22	(A)	(B)	(C)	(D)	46	(A)	(B)	(C)	(D)
23	(A)	(B)	(C)	(D)	47	(A)	(B)	(C)	(D)
24	(A)	(B)	(C)	(D)	48	(A)	(B)	(C)	(D)